The Destiny of the Damned

Arnold V Page

ISBN: 978-1-78364-504-6

www.obt.org.uk

THE OPEN BIBLE TRUST
Fordland Mount, Upper Basildon,
Reading, RG8 8LU, UK

The Destiny of the Damned

Contents

Introduction

INTRODUCTION

One of the hardest questions a believer in Christ is asked is, "How can a God of love allow so much evil and suffering to take place?" However, there is an even harder question to which many Christians have no satisfactory answer at all. It is, "How can a God of love deliberately torment unbelievers for ever in hell, especially if they have never heard of Jesus?" I hope that this little book will provide you with an answer to the second question at least.

Defining Words

> "When I use a word," Humpty Dumpty said, in rather a scornful tone, "it means just what I choose it to mean – neither more nor less."
>
> "The question is," said Alice, "whether you can make words mean so many different things."

Words are like curtains: they can shut out the light or let it in. In the original Hebrew and Greek of the Bible there are several different words for where people go when they die. Gehenna has a very different meaning from Sheol and Hades, and none of them means what is popularly thought of as hell. Nevertheless the Authorized (King James) Version translates all three words as 'hell'. This is confusing and it obscures the truth. Even my favourite Revised Standard Version translates Gehenna as hell.

Let's begin by drawing the curtains apart to see what these various words meant.

(i) Sheol

The Hebrew word 'Sheol' literally means 'the unseen state'. It is used as a synonym for death. After God had delivered David from all his enemies he sang,

> "the cords of Sheol entangled me, the snares of death confronted me." (2 Samuel 22.6)

Describing a 'loose woman' Proverbs 5.5 says,

> Her feet go down to death; her steps follow the path to Sheol.

However Sheol also seems to be regarded as a place beneath the earth.

> If I ascend to heaven, thou art there! If I make my bed in Sheol, thou art there! (Psalm 139.8)

> "Son of man, wail over the multitude of Egypt, and send them down … to the nether world, to those who have gone down to the Pit … The mighty chiefs shall speak of them, with their helpers, out of the midst of Sheol: 'They have come down, they lie still, the uncircumcised, slain by the sword.'" (Ezekiel 32.18,21)

In the Old Testament Sheol is everybody's destiny at death, at least until a day of judgment comes. In itself it is neither good nor bad.

> There the wicked cease from troubling, and there the weary are at rest. There the prisoners are at ease together;

they hear not the voice of the taskmaster. The small and the great are there, and the slave is free from his master. (Job 3.17-19)

(ii) The Pit

'The Pit' is an expression often used in the Old Testament as a synonym for Sheol.

> O Lord, thou hast brought up my soul from Sheol, restored me to life from among those gone down to the Pit. (Psalm 30.3)

To the evil city of Tyre God said,

> "… I will thrust you down with those who descend into the Pit, to the people of old, and I will make you to dwell in the nether world, among primeval ruins, with those who go down to the Pit, so that you will not be inhabited or have a place in the land of the living." (Ezekiel 26.20)

(iii) The dust

The Old Testament teaches that when we die our bodies decompose, but our spirits live on in a state akin to sleep, awaiting a day of judgment.

> … when thou takest away their breath, they die and return to their dust. (Psalm 104.29)

> … the dust returns to the earth as it was, and the spirit returns to God who gave it. (Ecclesiastes 12.7)

... for now shall I sleep in the dust. (Job 7.21 KJV)

... many of those who sleep in the dust of the earth shall awake, some to everlasting life, and some to shame and everlasting contempt. (Daniel 12.2)

With none of these Old Testament words is there any suggestion of punishment, flames or torture following death.

(iv) Hades

In the New Testament the Greek word *hadēs* literally means 'the unseen world'. Hades is the exact equivalent of Sheol. In Psalm 16.10 David had declared,

> ... thou dost not give me up to Sheol, or let thy godly one see the Pit.

When Peter quoted the Greek version of this same Psalm in Acts 2.27 he said,

> For thou wilt not abandon my soul to Hades, nor let thy Holy One see corruption.

Hades is Sheol.

Again it seems to be regarded as a place.
> "And you, Capernaum, will you be exalted to heaven? You shall be brought down to Hades." (Luke 10.15)

> "... I will build my church, and the powers of death (Greek: 'gates of Hades') shall not prevail against it." (Matthew 16.18)

However it is not identical to death, because Revelation 20.14 speaks of Death *and* Hades.

Hades is the place or state into which people enter at death to await the day of judgment; at least it is if they don't die as believers in Jesus Christ.

Hades will continue to exist until the day of judgment. After that, when no further people will be born and death will be abolished, Hades will be destroyed.

> And I saw the dead, great and small, standing before the throne, and books were opened … Death and Hades gave up the dead in them, and all were judged by what they had done. Then Death and Hades were thrown into the lake of fire. (Revelation 20.12-14)

(v) Gehenna

The other Greek word translated in the Authorized Version as 'hell' is *geenna*, which is normally pronounced and written as 'Gehenna'.

Gehenna was a rubbish tip outside Jerusalem, a place more accurately known as the Valley of Hinnom. It's still there, to the south-west of the old city of Jerusalem, but nowadays it's mostly covered by grass. It is not some place 'under the earth', neither is it the opposite of heaven. Whenever Jesus used the word 'Gehenna' he meant simply 'the rubbish tip'. Bible commentators generally agree that the valley was used to dispose of animal carcasses, rubbish and perhaps also the corpses of executed criminals. They were either burned up or eaten by maggots, so it was an appropriate word for a place of destruction. In the first century one corner was used as a proper burial ground, and the Jewish historian Josephus recorded that the tomb of Annas the high priest was located there.

(vi) Hell

The English word 'hell' originally meant much the same as Sheol or Hades, the netherworld of the dead. But in the Middle Ages it came to mean something far worse. The terrifying paintings of hell produced during mediaeval and Renaissance times reflected and reinforced a belief that the final destiny of the wicked is to be tormented for ever in the presence of the devil and his angels. However Michelangelo's fresco of the *Last Judgment* on the wall behind the altar in the Sistine Chapel is particularly frightening, not because it depicts horrible demons toasting human beings for supper as some earlier paintings did, but because the terrified men and women on the wrong side of Jesus at Judgment Day appear so lifelike. Of course it was in the interests of the mediaeval church to propagate such beliefs and at the same time to teach that salvation was found only in the church. It ensured faithful church attendance and full offering plates!

There is no evidence in the Bible that hell as it is popularly envisaged is a real place at all. Genesis says that in the beginning God created the heavens and the earth, not heaven and earth and hell. Still less is hell a place inhabited by Satan and his demons. In the book of Job, Satan is either talking to God in heaven or poking around on the earth. Paul wrote that the spiritual hosts of wickedness dwell in the heavenly places (Ephesians 6.12), and Revelation chapter 12 says that Satan and his angels will be in heaven, along with Michael and other angels, until Resurrection Day. The same chapter then says that after Resurrection Day Satan and his angels will be thrown out of heaven and come down to the earth. Nowhere does the Bible say that Satan inhabits a fiery place called hell.

So when Jesus says in Mark chapter 9, verses 47 and 48,

> "And if your eye causes you to sin, pluck it out; it is better for you to enter the kingdom of God with one eye than with two eyes to be thrown into hell, where their worm does not die, and the fire is not quenched,"

the word translated as 'hell' is 'Gehenna', and he was simply saying, "It is better for you to enter the kingdom of God with one eye than with two eyes to be thrown on to the rubbish tip…"

With regard to the undying worm and unquenchable fire, Jesus was quoting the last verse of the book of the prophet Isaiah. God had been telling Isaiah what life would be like when Israel's enemies had finally been defeated. He concluded,

> And they shall go forth and look on the dead bodies of the men that have rebelled against me; for their worm shall not die, their fire shall not be quenched, and they shall be an abhorrence to all flesh. (Isaiah 66.24)

It's vital to see that this verse says the bodies of the rebellious men being consumed by worms and fire were dead bodies, not living bodies. There is no hint in this passage that the men who had rebelled against the Lord were somehow going to live in torment for ever, rather the opposite. The idea was that the worms wouldn't die and the fire wouldn't go out until the dead bodies had been entirely consumed.

Similarly, in Jeremiah 17.27 the Lord declared to the ancient Jews,

> "... if you do not listen to me... then will I kindle a fire in [Jerusalem's] gates, and it shall devour the palaces of Jerusalem and shall not be quenched."

That prophecy of Jerusalem's destruction was fulfilled when the Babylonians torched the city. However, the fire they lit is not still burning today, so was the prophecy wrong? No. The Lord's word to Jeremiah never meant that the fire would burn for ever. It meant that no one would be able to quench its flames until they had completed their task of destruction.

It was these Old Testament pictures that Jesus was recalling in order to make his vivid point that it is better to make any sacrifice necessary to eliminate sin and enter the kingdom of God than to face the dreadful alternative of an ignominious, complete, final and permanent end to one's life from which there could be no escape.

It's true that Revelation chapters 19, 20 and 21 speak of a 'lake of fire', into which will be thrown Death, Hades, Satan and everyone whose name is not written in the book of life. However it's no more necessary to think that this will be a literal lake burning with fire than it is to think that the antichrist will be a beast with ten horns and seven heads as Revelation 13.1 says he will be.[1] When

---

[1] Some Bible commentators such as William Barclay take the view that the beast does not even symbolize a man, but the Roman Empire. That may have been John's intention, but even if it was I believe it will find a more significant fulfilment in the

Jesus warned his hearers that the unrighteous would be thrown into Gehenna he did not mean it literally. The Valley of Hinnom is probably no more than half a mile square, so there wouldn't be room in it for every unbeliever or wicked person who has ever lived to be burned up or eaten up there. Jesus used the word 'Gehenna' metaphorically, so John could equally have used the phrase 'the lake of fire' metaphorically. After all, you can't literally throw death anywhere, let alone into a lake, yet according to John death was thrown into the lake of fire (Revelation 20.14). Throwing death into a lake of fire was merely a symbolical way of saying that death would come to an end, as indeed Revelation 21.4 says it will. So when John wrote that those whose names were not written in the book of life would follow Death and Hades into the lake of fire, he was saying in a symbolical way that they too would come to an end. The 'lake of fire' is a metaphor for a place of destruction. It doesn't have to be a real place at all.

coming 'man of lawlessness' whom Paul spoke of in 2 Thessalonians 2.3.

THE BASIS OF JUDGMENT

THE BASIS OF JUDGMENT

(i) A matter of life or death

> "I call heaven and earth to witness against you this day, that I have set before you life and death, blessing and curse; therefore choose life, that you and your descendants may live, loving the Lord your God, obeying his voice, and cleaving to him; for that means life to you and length of days, that you may dwell in the land which the Lord swore to your fathers, to Abraham, to Isaac, and to Jacob, to give them." (Deuteronomy 30.19,20)

> The wages of sin is death, but the free gift of God is eternal life in Christ Jesus our Lord. (Romans 6.23)

In both the Old and the New Testaments God gives us a choice between life and death. In the Old Testament life meant a good life in this world; in the New Testament it means an even better life in the world to come. In both cases the alternative is death. The question for those who believe in Christ is, who gets to live for ever and who doesn't?

The passage from Deuteronomy actually gives us a clue. God wants to populate his eternal kingdom of righteousness with people who want to do his will because they love him. He doesn't want people who have to be forced to obey him, and he doesn't want people who refuse to obey him. He wants to have a gloriously happy world in which everyone loves him and everyone loves each other perfectly. And the reason he wants this is because that's how he loves us.

In the New Testament the passage from Romans tells us that God will freely grant eternal life to anyone who believes in Jesus for salvation and submits to Jesus as Lord. This is because through the work of the indwelling Holy Spirit Jesus can make us fit to live in the kingdom of God. (See Romans 8.1-4.)

But what about people who want nothing to do with Jesus? Or people who have never even heard of him? How will their fate be decided? It depends on whether they are mules, wild boars, sheep or goats!

(ii) Mules

> And this is the judgment, that the light has come into the world, and men loved darkness rather than light, because their deeds were evil. (John 3.19)

Through his Son Jesus Christ, God invites everyone to live for ever in his everlasting kingdom. And Jesus gave his life to make this possible. So how can anyone know this yet turn his back on Jesus? Anyone who knows about this amazing offer yet nevertheless rejects it is like a stubborn mule, a stubborn and tragically foolish mule. For God's word is unambiguous:

> He who believes in [Jesus] is not condemned; he who does not believe is condemned already, because he has not believed in the name of the only Son of God. (John 3.18)

John wasn't writing about people who don't believe in Jesus because they have never heard of him: he meant people who do know about Jesus yet still refuse to believe in him. Unless they repent before they die, the verdict for them on the day of judgment has already been decided: it will be condemnation! Please, please don't be a mule!

(iii) Wild boars

Wild boars represent people who wilfully engage in all kinds of evil, who consistently oppose the will of God, and who live chiefly for themselves. Their behaviour is described in at least four places in the New Testament: Romans 1.29-31, 1 Corinthians 6.9-11, Galatians 5.19-21 and Ephesians 5.3-5.

Common sense tells us that a man who has raped innocent girls or gassed Jews or plundered a firm's assets before leaving it in bankruptcy is not likely to be granted citizenship in the kingdom of God. Jesus said,

> "The Son of man will send his angels, and they will gather out of his kingdom all causes of sin and all evildoers, and throw them into the furnace of fire." (Matthew 13.41,42)

Unless such people truly repent before they die they won't inherit eternal life.

However the references listed above include behaviour that seems to be far less serious. Some of it wouldn't be regarded as sin at all by many people. For example: gossiping, boasting and breaking promises; premarital sex, adultery and homosexual activities; greed, drunkenness, anger, jealousy; and even plain selfishness! God's word clearly states that deliberately continuing in any such behaviour without repentance will exclude people from his coming kingdom. And this includes those who regard themselves as Christians! "I warn you, as I warned you before, that those who do such things shall not inherit the kingdom of God" Paul wrote to the churches in Galatia (Galatians 5.21).

> Do not be deceived; neither the immoral ... nor robbers will inherit the kingdom of God. And such were some of you. But you were washed, you were sanctified, you were justified (made righteous) in the name of the Lord Jesus Christ and in the Spirit of our God. (1 Corinthians 6.9,11)

> Let no one deceive you... it is because of these things that the wrath of God comes upon the sons of disobedience. (Ephesians 5.6)

Thankfully it's not a case of 'one strike and you're out'. The apostle Peter wasn't perfect, and Paul admitted that he wasn't. We don't have to be perfect, but we must *want* to be. We cannot love God and at the same time want to continue in a lifestyle that he has told us he hates. Our heavenly Father is seeking people who hunger and thirst after righteousness. Righteousness is simply living how he wants us to. If we don't want to live as God wants us to live, how can we expect to be given the right to live in the kingdom of righteousness? "Why do you call me, 'Lord, Lord,' and not do what I tell you?" Jesus demanded (Luke 6.46). Would *you* want to spend eternity surrounded by gossips or by people eaten up by jealousy?

Where we find it hard to change, that is just where Jesus can help us. The very reason he came into the world was to deliver us from our sins, to make us fit to live in God's kingdom. "...God is at work in you, both to will and to work for his good pleasure," Philippians 2.13 says. He does this through his Spirit living in us.

... the fruit of the Spirit is love, joy, peace, patience, kindness, goodness, faithfulness, gentleness, self-control; against such there is no law. (Galatians 5.22,23)

Jesus knows we can find it difficult to change, but he can change us if we'll let him.

"... if the Son makes you free, you will be free indeed." (John 8.36)

So check out those four lists of unrighteous behaviour in Romans, Corinthians, Galatians and Ephesians. Agree with God's word. Ask Jesus to set you free from everything you read there that is hateful to God. Persist in prayer until you have the victory! Don't be a wild boar!

(iv) Sheep and goats

Sheep and goats stand for people who die never having heard of Jesus Christ, or with only a limited or distorted knowledge of him. They are not mules who have rejected his help, nor wild boars whose actions and lifestyle disqualify them from citizenship in the kingdom of God. They are simply people who have or have not loved their neighbours as themselves!

"When the Son of man comes in his glory, and all the angels with him, then he will sit on his glorious throne. Before him will be gathered all the nations, and he will separate them one from another as a shepherd separates the sheep from the goats, and he will place the sheep at his right hand, but the goats at the left. Then the King will say to those at his right hand, 'Come, O blessed of my Father, inherit the kingdom prepared for you from the foundation of the world; for I was hungry and you gave me food, I was thirsty and you gave me drink, I was a stranger and you welcomed me, I was naked and you clothed me, I was sick and you visited me, I was in prison and you came to me.' Then the righteous will answer him, 'Lord, when did we see thee hungry and feed thee, or thirsty and give thee drink? And when did we see thee a stranger and welcome thee, or naked and clothe thee? And when did we see thee sick or in prison and visit thee?' And the King will answer them, 'Truly, I say to you, as you did it to one of the least of these my brethren, you did it to me.' Then he will say to those at his left hand, 'Depart from me, you cursed, into the eternal fire prepared for the devil and his angels; for I was hungry and you gave me no food, I was thirsty and you gave me no drink, I was a stranger and you did not welcome me, naked and you did not clothe me, sick and in prison and you did not visit me.' Then they also will answer, 'Lord, when did we see thee hungry or thirsty or a stranger or naked or sick or in prison, and did not minister to thee?' Then he will answer them, 'Truly, I say to you, as you did it not to one of the least of these, you did it not to me.' And they will go away into eternal punishment, but the righteous into eternal life." (Matthew 25.31-46)

Some people understand Christ's 'brethren' in this passage to be Christians, people who have been born again as children of God and have thereby become Christ's brothers and sisters. But if that's so then people who had no contact with Christians could never qualify as sheep by helping them. The Bible commentator William Barclay understands the word 'brethren' differently.

If we really wish to delight a parent's heart, if we really wish to move him to gratitude, the best way to do it is to help his child. God is the great Father; and the way to delight the heart of God is to help his children, our fellow men.[2]

The kind of help God is looking for is simple help that anyone can give. And it must not be motivated merely by the hope of a reward. Barclay continued,

Those who helped did not think that they were helping Christ and thus piling up eternal merit … It was the natural, instinctive, quite uncalculating reaction of the loving heart. Whereas … the attitude of those who failed to help was, "If we had known it was you we would gladly have helped; but we thought it was only some common man who was not worth helping."

What a high bar this parable sets for people who haven't put their trust in Jesus for salvation! The goats will be condemned, not because of what they've done, but because of what they've not done.

Yet Jesus sets an even higher bar for those of us who *have* put our trust in him. "A new commandment I give to you, that you love one another; even as I have loved you, that you also love one another," he said (John 13.34). Thankfully by the grace of God our salvation in Christ is secure, but that must never lead us into complacency. Instead God's grace should motivate us 'to lead a life worthy of our calling', to aim for 'the measure of the stature

---

[2]   *The Gospel of Matthew, Volume 2*. W. Barclay, The Daily Study Bible, revised edition, The Saint Andrew Press,1975, p.326.

of the fullness of Christ', and to 'press on to perfection' (Ephesians 4.1; Ephesians 4.13; Philippians 3.12). Nothing less should satisfy us (Matthew 5.6).

(v) The righteous judge

God has appointed his Son Jesus to be the judge, and his judgment will be totally just (John 5.22; 2 Timothy 4.8).

- Jesus will take into account people's understanding of the Father's will. In a parable about disobedient servants Jesus said, "…that servant who knew his master's will, but did not make ready or act according to his will, shall receive a severe beating. But he who did not know, and did what deserved a beating, shall receive a light beating." (Luke 12.47,48)

- He will look at what people do rather than what they say. The son who did his father's will was the son who went to work in his father's vineyard even though he had said he wouldn't, rather than his brother who said he would go and then didn't. (Matthew 21.28-31)

- Yet he will look beyond what people do into their motivation. 1 Samuel 16.7 says, "…man looks on the outward appearance, but the Lord looks on the heart." A wealthy person who donates large sums to charity may look good to us but not to the Lord if his actions are motivated merely by the hope of gaining a peerage or senatorship. "Do you love me, Peter?" Jesus asked after Peter had badly let him down. In the end, what matters most is what's in our hearts.

(vi) Judgment by works?

In John 5.24 and John 5.21 Jesus declares that anyone who hears his teaching and believes it will not come in for judgment at all. "Truly, truly, I say to you, he who hears my word and believes him who sent me, has eternal life; he does not come into judgment, but has [already] passed from death to life... For as the Father raises the dead and gives them life, so also the Son gives life to whom he will." In other words, those who believe in Jesus will be raised from the dead before the day of judgment comes and will then live for ever. This resurrection of believers is what Revelation 20.5 calls 'the first resurrection'.

Then in John 5.28,29 Jesus turns his attention to everyone else and the day of judgment. "The hour is coming when all who are in the tombs [and have not therefore been raised from the dead already] will hear his voice and come forth, those who have done good, to the resurrection of life, and those who have done evil, to the resurrection of judgment." Here Jesus is speaking of a second resurrection that will occur at the end of his thousand-year reign on the present earth. (See Revelation 20.5 again.) He says that this resurrection of everyone who has not believed in him will result in either *life* or *condemnation*. (The word translated in verse 29 as 'judgment' can also mean 'condemnation', as in Hebrews 10.27.) For these people judgment will not be on the basis of whether they have believed Jesus's teaching, for they may never have heard of him. It will be on the basis, Jesus says, of whether they have 'done good' or have 'done evil' during their lifetime. In other words, judgment for those who have not heard his teaching will be according to their works.

This is confirmed in the description of judgment day given in Revelation 20.11-15.

... books were opened. Also another book was opened, which is the book of life. And the dead were judged by what was written in the books, by what they had done... all were judged by what they had done... and if anyone's name was not found written in the book of life, he was thrown into the lake of fire.

Even the apostle Paul says that God 'will render to every man according to his works' (Romans 2.6). So why then does he say in Ephesians, '...by grace you have been saved through faith; and this is not your own doing, it is the gift of God, *not because of works*, lest any man should boast' (Ephesians 2.8,9)? It's because in the letter to the Ephesians Paul was addressing Christians, people who had heard the gospel and had put their faith in Jesus Christ. In the amazing love and grace of God, whatever we have done or have not done becomes irrelevant the moment we put our faith in Jesus to save us. Our works, whether good or bad, no longer count for or against us. We do not have to earn our citizenship in the kingdom of God. We have become God's sons and daughters, and as members of God's family citizenship is now ours by right. Praise the Lord!

Naturally this raises the question: can believers therefore be as wicked as they want without fear of condemnation? In reality the question doesn't make sense because believers in Christ will not want to be wicked. The Bible says that people who truly accept Jesus as Saviour and Lord and live by the power of his Spirit will fulfil the requirements of God's law. They will love God and their neighbour and will no longer want to rebel against God's will:

> For God has done what the law, weakened by the flesh, could not do: [by] sending his own Son in the likeness of sinful flesh and for sin, he condemned sin in the flesh, in

order that the just requirement of the law might be fulfilled in us, who walk not according to the flesh but according to the Spirit. (Romans 8.3,4)

THE FATE OF THE UNRIGHTEOUS IN THE NEW TESTAMENT

THE FATE OF THE UNRIGHTEOUS IN THE NEW TESTAMENT

So what will be the fate of the unrighteous? The New Testament mentions five different fates at Judgment Day for those who are not granted eternal life in the kingdom of God:

- Death, destruction or perishing (22 times)
- Gehenna, the Gehenna of fire, fire (26 times)
- Weeping and gnashing of teeth (7 times)
- Punishment (4 times)
- Torment (3 times)

We'll look at each of these in turn.

Death, destruction or perishing

(i) Death

The New Testament speaks of two deaths, as well as two resurrections. The first death is when we die naturally. People who die as believers in Christ will then be resurrected on Resurrection Day. Their spirit will rejoin a resurrected and immortal body and they will never die again. Other people will be resurrected on the day of judgment. On that day those who are not invited into God's kingdom will die a second time, but this time both their body and spirit will die. This is called the second death. It is the final end of life.

> Blessed and holy is he who shares in the first resurrection! Over such the second death has no power … (Revelation 20.6)

Jesus described this second death as the death of body and soul.

> "Do not fear those who kill the body but cannot kill the soul; rather fear him who can destroy both soul and body in hell." (Matthew 10.28)

So when Paul wrote, "… the wages of sin is death, but the free gift of God is eternal life in Christ Jesus …" (Romans 6.23), he was writing about the second, final death. He was not writing about the first death, because even Christians have to die in body, at least until Resurrection Day is upon us. Jesus does not save us from the first death, but he will save us from the second death by grace, if we truly trust in him as our Saviour and Lord.

(ii) Destruction

In the Authorized Version of the Bible the English words 'destroy', 'destroyed' or 'destroying' occur about *500 times*, and they always mean the annihilation of whatever is destroyed, not its continuing existence. So when these words are applied to the final destiny of the ungodly, that is just what they must mean: their annihilation. We must not change the meaning of a word just because we'd prefer it to mean something else.

When Jesus said, "Do not fear those who kill the body but cannot kill the soul; rather fear him who can destroy both soul and body in hell" he was saying that men can *kill* us (*apokteinai*) but God can *destroy* us (*apolesai*). *Apolesai* is stronger than *apokteinai*. According to the authoritative Grimm-Thayer Greek-English lexicon, *apolesai* means 'to destroy, i.e. to put out of the way entirely, abolish, put an end to, ruin'. So Jesus was saying that while men can merely kill the body in the first death, God can destroy both the body and soul in the second death, bringing us to an end entirely. Both are cases of destruction, but God's destruction will be complete destruction.

Peter uses a different Greek word for destruction in 2 Peter 3.7:

> ... the heavens and earth that now exist have been stored up for fire, being kept until the day of judgment and destruction of ungodly men.

Here the word for destruction, *apōleias*, means 'the destroying or utter destruction of something or someone'. Peter says that the destiny of ungodly men is to be utterly destroyed.

In 2 Thessalonians 1.5-9 Paul writes about what he calls

> ... the righteous judgment of God... when the Lord Jesus is revealed from heaven with his mighty angels in flaming fire, inflicting vengeance upon those who do not know God and upon those who do not obey the Gospel of our Lord Jesus. They shall suffer the punishment of eternal destruction and exclusion from (away from) the presence of the Lord and from the glory of his might.

Here Paul uses another Greek word for 'destruction', but it means much the same as the others. *Olethros* means 'ruin, destruction, death'. Paul unambiguously states that the coming vengeance and punishment for the ungodly will be eternal and permanent 'ruin, destruction and death'.

Destruction means destruction. None of these verses suggests everlasting existence, punishment or torment. What awaits the ungodly at the day of judgment is not everlasting punishment but permanent destruction. It couldn't be clearer that the alternative to eternal life is to perish, to be blotted out, to be utterly destroyed, to cease to exist for ever.

(iii) Perishing

The other word used for the destiny of the ungodly is 'perish'. John 3.16, possibly the most famous verse in the Bible, presents everyone with a choice between eternal life and perishing.

> For God so loved the world that he gave his only Son, that whoever believes in him should not perish but have eternal life.

According to the lexicon, the Greek word used in this verse for 'perish', *apolētai*, means 'to destroy, i.e. to put out of the way entirely, abolish, put an end to, ruin'. The same word is used many times in the New Testament. Old wineskins 'perish', the world as it was first created 'perished' in the Flood, the disciples thought they would 'perish' in a storm on the Sea of Galilee, those who take the sword will 'perish' by the sword. In every case 'perish' means to come to an end, to be destroyed, to die. So John 3.16 says that people who do not receive eternal life will come to an end, be destroyed, die. There is not the slightest suggestion that they will continue to live for ever, still less in torment.

(iv) Immortal souls?

Some people believe that our souls are immortal, which means by definition that they cannot die. If our souls really were immortal then even God could not destroy them, any more than he could make a four-sided triangle or a foot ruler that's three-feet long. But the idea that our souls are immortal comes from Plato and other ancient Greek philosophers, not the Bible. The Bible does say that God 'has put eternity into man's mind' (Ecclesiastes 3.11) but all that means is that we have an innate sense that we were meant to live for ever. Jesus said,

> "… do not fear those (i.e. men) who kill the body but cannot kill the soul; rather fear him (i.e. God) who can destroy both *soul* and body in hell (Gehenna)." (Matthew 10.28)

Gehenna, the Gehenna of fire, fire

Jesus frequently said that the ungodly would be cast into Gehenna or into eternal fire.

> "…if your right hand causes you to sin, cut it off and throw it away; it is better that you lose one of your members than that your whole body go into hell (Gehenna)." (Matthew 5.30)

> "…if your eye causes you to sin, pluck it out and throw it away; it is better for you to enter life with one eye than

with two eyes to be thrown into the hell (Gehenna) of fire."
(Matthew 18.9)

"…if your hand or foot causes you to sin, cut it off and
throw it away; it is better for you to enter life maimed or
lame than with two hands or two feet to be thrown into the
eternal fire." (Matthew 18.8)

John the Baptist employed the concept of fire too:

"… he will clear his threshing floor and gather his wheat
into the granary, but the chaff he will burn with
unquenchable fire." (Matthew 3.12)

Just as the rubbish tip in the Valley of Hinnom was a place for
getting rid of refuse, so a fire is the ultimate way of destroying
something. In earlier centuries when nearly all homes were heated
by coal fires, anything that could burn would be thrown into the
fire to destroy it. If a woman received an unwanted circular she
would throw it in the fire. If a man wrote a new will and asked
what he should do with the old one he would be told, "Throw it in
the fire". That is what people always did when they needed to
destroy something; when they wanted to be certain that it did not
continue to exist.

The many verses in the gospel about Gehenna and fire mean that
the destiny of the ungodly is to be destroyed.

Weeping and gnashing of teeth

On six occasions in Matthew's Gospel and once in Luke's Gospel
Jesus prophesies that evildoers will weep and gnash their teeth
when they meet their doom. For example;

"... many will come from east and west and sit at table with Abraham, Isaac, and Jacob in the kingdom of heaven, while the sons of the kingdom will be thrown into the outer darkness; there men will weep and gnash their teeth." (Matthew 8.11,12)

Weeping is an expression of grief. Teeth gnashing is always associated in the Old Testament with anger or hatred. It's not obvious whether the anger or hatred of the teeth-gnashers will be directed at God for excluding them from his kingdom, or at themselves for being so foolish as to ignore God and his will and thereby forfeit eternal life, but I think it will be the latter. In other words, they will be stricken with grief and remorse.

There is a long description of such remorse in the *Wisdom of Solomon*, a Jewish book written around the time of Jesus. The passage begins,

> When the unrighteous see [the righteous in bliss], they will be shaken with dreadful fear, and they will be amazed at the unexpected salvation of the righteous. They will speak to one another in repentance, and in anguish of spirit they will groan, and say, "These are persons whom we once held in derision and made a byword of reproach – fools that we were!" (Wisdom of Solomon 5.1-5)

Another Jewish book of that time, 2 Esdras, says that there will be a week's delay after judgment, which will give the wicked an opportunity to reflect on their wrongdoing and their consequent loss of eternal life, as well as for the righteous to rejoice! (2 Esdras 7.101).

So it may be that at the last judgment those whose names are not found in the book of life will be given time to reflect on their folly in ignoring God, in living selfishly, in doing bad things and in not believing the truth. When they realize that God really is going to make a new and perfect earth in which they could have lived for ever, then truly they will weep and gnash their teeth.

As I said at the beginning, most Christians assume that this will continue for ever in hell. But it is not obvious from any of these passages how long the weeping and teeth gnashing will last, nor where it will take place. Not one of these passages says that it will continue for ever. Although Jesus repeatedly uses the word 'there', in three cases it is in 'the outer darkness', twice in 'the furnace of fire', once 'with the hypocrites', and once somewhere away from Jesus and excluded from the kingdom of God. These differences in location suggest that Jesus did not intend the various expressions of location to be understood literally. Job 18.18 and Job 8.13 in the Authorized Version show that 'outer darkness' and 'with the hypocrites' were simply expressions for separation from God. 'The furnace' was a metaphor for destruction, set in the context of a parable about harvest time. In Matthew 13.40-42 the destination of evildoers was in 'the furnace of fire' because that is where weeds were put.

> "Just as the weeds are gathered and burned with fire, so will it be at the close of the age … they will gather out of his kingdom all causes of sin and all evildoers, and throw them into the furnace of fire; there men will weep and gnash their teeth."

(Evidently farmers in the first century weren't concerned about global warming!)

Nevertheless people commonly equate the phrases 'outer darkness', 'with the hypocrites', 'the furnace of fire' and 'thrust out of the kingdom' with the traditional idea of hell. They conclude that the wicked will continue to weep and gnash their teeth in some kind of fire for ever. They come to this conclusion in spite of the fact that Jesus said the alternative to eternal life is to *perish* (John 3.16), and that after the day of judgment and the creation of a new heaven and earth *everything* that remains will be united in and with Christ (Revelation 21.4; Ephesians 1.10). That can never be true if most people will continue to exist in an everlasting state of remorse, separated from Christ. So what did Jesus mean by 'there'?

All seven of these passages are principally about the coming separation of 'good' and 'bad' people at the end of this age, and about the grief and remorse the 'bad' people will experience on learning that they have been excluded from the kingdom of God. Instead of being invited to sit at table in the kingdom of God they are thrust outside; instead of being gathered into the barn they are burned outside in a furnace; instead of being put into vessels for use as good fish they are thrown back into the sea; instead of being invited into the house they are shut out of it; instead of being a guest at a wedding feast they are thrown out into the night. Their remorse is not because of where they end up, which Jesus left deliberately vague. They are not weeping because everything outside is dark. They are not grinding their teeth because of burning flames. Their remorse is because of where they have *not* ended up, i.e. in the kingdom of God! The passage in Luke's Gospel makes this particularly clear:

> "When once the householder has risen up and shut the door, you will begin to stand outside and to knock at the door, saying, 'Lord, open to us.' ... But he will say, 'I tell

you, I do not know where you come from; depart from me, all you workers of iniquity!' There you will weep and gnash your teeth, when you see Abraham and Isaac and Jacob and all the prophets in the kingdom of God and you yourselves thrust out." (Luke 13.25-28)

The decision to exclude the unrighteous from the kingdom of God will be announced at the judgment seat of Christ (Matthew 25.31,32; Revelation 20.11-13). It is *there* that the unrighteous will learn their fate, so it is *there* that they will weep and gnash their teeth in consequence.

All we can say with confidence from these seven passages about teeth and tears is that at the day of judgment evildoers will bitterly regret the life they have led when they discover that they are to be excluded from everlasting life in the kingdom of God. That is the essence of what Jesus was teaching. And he did this in order to urge his hearers – and all of us who read his words today – not to end up in that same terrible state when we discover that everything Jesus taught really was true; and that because we ignored his teaching and left God out of our lives we have irrevocably forfeited the possibility of living for ever in a world beyond our wildest dreams, but instead we shall be destroyed like weeds in a furnace.

It was out of love for you and me that Jesus issued these dire warnings. Charles Wesley expressed this in a hymn[3] addressed to anyone who has not yet asked Jesus to be their Saviour. The words are based on Ezekiel 33.11:

---

[3]   Hymn no. 327 in *The Methodist Hymnbook*, Methodist Conference Office, London, 1933.

Sinners turn; why will ye die?
      God, your Maker, asks you why.
God, who did your being give,
      made you with Himself to live,
He the fatal cause demands,
      asks the work of His own hands:
Why, ye reckless creatures,
      why will you cross His love, and die?

Punishment

(i) Matthew 25.46

In Matthew 25.46, Jesus ended his teaching on the last judgment by describing the fate of the 'goats'.

> "And they will go away into eternal punishment, but the righteous into eternal life."

In the Authorized Version the fate of the goats sounds even worse:

> "And these shall go away into *everlasting* punishment: but the righteous into life eternal."

At first sight the word 'everlasting' seems to contradict the fact that the alternative to eternal life is, as we have seen, to perish (John 3.16). How can anyone perish everlastingly? *Aiōnios*, the word that is translated in the Authorized Version as both 'eternal' and 'everlasting', has several possible meanings. It is the adjective from the noun *aiōn*. (The English version of this is 'aeon'.) *Aiōn* can mean 'life and breath, a human lifetime, an unbroken age, a historical age, the age or ages to come, perpetuity of time, or eternity past present and future'. So *aiōnios* can mean 'everlasting', but it can equally mean 'the kind that will exist in the age to come' or even 'permanent'. In Matthew 10.28 Jesus said that the punishment awaiting sinners will be the destruction of both their bodies and souls. In other words, it will be a final death from which there can be no resurrection, an eternal death as distinct from a temporal death, the permanent kind of death that will exist in the age to come, not the mere physical death of the body which will be brought back to life to face judgment. And that is why Jesus described the forthcoming punishment of the unrighteous as eternal.

Precisely the same point is made in *The New Bible Commentary Revised* [4]:

> *Eternal punishment* and *eternal life* are not necessarily the same in duration. *Eternal* (Gk. *aiōnios*) simply refers to the age to come and makes the point that the division is final for men's destiny.

(ii) 2 Thessalonians 1.8,9

> … those who do not know God and those who do not obey the gospel of our Lord Jesus…shall suffer the punishment of eternal destruction and exclusion from the presence of the Lord … (2 Thessalonians 1.8,9)

Here Paul clarifies what Jesus meant by punishment in Matthew 25.46. It will be destruction, the final destruction of the ungodly and their resulting permanent exclusion from the Lord's presence.

---

[4] *The New Bible Commentary Revised.* D.Guthrie and others. Inter-Varsity Press, Leicester, 1970, p.846

(iii) 2 Peter 2.9

> ... the Lord knows how to rescue the godly from trial, and to keep the unrighteous under punishment until the day of judgment ... (2 Peter 2.9)

As it is translated in the Revised Standard Version this verse is rather confusing. However, the Greek word *kolazomenous*, translated as 'under punishment', can equally well be translated as 'under restraint'. That is how it should be translated here, as well as in Acts 4.21, where the chief concern of the Jewish rulers was not to punish Peter and John, but to curb or restrain them from preaching the gospel.

(iv) Hebrews 10.28,29

> A man who has violated the law of Moses dies without mercy at the testimony of two or three witnesses. How much worse punishment do you think will be deserved by the man who has spurned the Son of God ... (Hebrews 10.28,29)

This is the final verse in the New Testament that speaks of 'punishment' following the day of judgment. But once again the punishment spoken of is destruction rather than some perpetual torment. The writer is writing about believers in Christ who deliberately turn their back on him and actually become adversaries to the Christian faith. In the two previous verses he describes what their punishment will be:

> For if we sin deliberately after receiving the knowledge of the truth, there no longer remains a sacrifice for sins, but a

fearful prospect of judgment, and a fury of fire which will consume the adversaries.

(v) The painful scales of justice

There are two final questions about punishment that need answering. Will the destined destruction of the ungodly be painful, and if so will it be equally painful for everyone?

A child's instinctive cry, "It's not fair," arises from a conviction we all have that injustice is wrong. The other day I was reading about a massacre that took place in the Kandhamal district of eastern India in August 2008. More than 90 Christians were murdered by Hindu nationalists. 5,600 houses were looted and burned, and some 295 churches and other places of worship were destroyed. Yet in spite of over 3,300 complaints to the police almost 90% of the known perpetrators were acquitted. Every molecule of morality and quark of conscience screams out that this was wrong; that at the very least the perpetrators should have been brought to justice and punished. To allow them to pursue their normal life scot-free, Hindu-free or any other kind of free while most of their victims have received no compensation is undeniably "not fair".

In contrast, the Bible tells us that the Lord God *is* fair: he will do what is right. *"Shall not the Judge of all the earth do right?"* asked Abraham, and the Lord evidently agreed with him (Genesis 18.25). As the righteous judge, the Lord assures us that either in this life or the next he will repay wrongdoing. *"Vengeance is mine: I will repay, says the Lord"* (Romans 12.19).

The principle that God laid down for justice on earth was that wrongdoing must be punished, and that it must be punished in proportion to the wrongdoing itself:

> He who kills a man shall be put to death. He who kills a beast shall make it good, life for life. When a man causes a disfigurement in his neighbour, as he has done it shall be done to him, fracture for fracture, eye for eye, tooth for tooth. As he has disfigured a man, he shall be disfigured. (Leviticus 24.17-20)

The idea that the punishment should fit the crime may sound barbarous in our gentler culture, but imagine how merciful it would have sounded only a few centuries ago when a man could be hanged just for stealing a lamb! If then the Lord is going to be true to his own principle of punishing wrongdoers in proportion to their crimes, how could he make all evildoers suffer exactly the same fate at the day of judgment, particularly if that fate were merely to bring their lives to a quiet and peaceful end? How could it be just for men like Stalin, Hitler, Ivan the Terrible, Vlad the Impaler and others like them to suffer exactly the same fate on Judgment Day as a little old lady who has merely lived rather selfishly?

We have already seen that the unrighteous will experience a period of remorse before their final destruction. But the Bible goes further than this. Its unchanging image of the means of that final destruction is the image of fire. (See Malachi 4.1; Matthew 3.12 & 13.40,41; 2 Peter 3.7-10; Revelation 20.15.) Being burnt to death doesn't take for ever but it doesn't happen instantaneously either, and furthermore it is extremely painful. So while the Bible firmly declares that the destiny of the damned is their final extinction, I believe that prior to this they will have to suffer in proportion to the suffering that they themselves have inflicted.

I know that God is merciful and kind, and that 'he does not willingly afflict or grieve the sons of men.' (Lamentations 3.33) Nevertheless that is exactly what he does do when it is necessary for the sake of justice. He destroyed all but eight inhabitants of Sodom and Gomorrah with fire and brimstone, and all but eight inhabitants of the earth with a universal flood. Following the world-wide evacuation of believers in Christ on Resurrection Day, Revelation chapter 16 tells us that God is going to pour out his wrath on those who remain during the last three and a half years before Christ returns. If those remaining inhabitants of the earth are to suffer foul sores, scorching heat and hailstones weighing a hundredweight, how could it be just for men and women who lived earlier in history like Pol Pot, who caused the death of a third of Cambodia's population, to be rewarded on the day of judgment with nothing worse than a quick and painless end?

So the all-important question arises: did Jesus himself support the idea that wrongdoers will be punished in proportion to their guilt? Absolutely!

> "Woe to you, Chorazin! Woe to you, Bethsaida! For if the mighty works done in you had been done in Tyre and Sidon, they would have repented long ago in sackcloth and ashes. But I tell you, it shall be more tolerable on the day of judgment for Tyre and Sidon than for you." (Matthew 11.21,22)

> "That servant who knew his master's will, but did not make ready or act according to his will, shall receive a

severe beating. But he who did not know, and did what deserved a beating, shall receive a light beating." (Luke 12.47,48)

It is only my fancy, but if the fires of God's judgment have to destroy the evil in men's hearts as well as their bodies and souls, it may necessarily take longer to burn them up if their deeds have been especially evil. I presume that the longer it takes the more painful their destruction will be.

(vi) Conclusion

The word 'punishment' in connection with the final destiny of the damned is mentioned only four times in the New Testament. It is defined as their destruction or their consumption by fire. Where it is described as 'eternal' it means that it will be permanent and final: the resulting death of the unrighteous will include their total destruction, body and soul.

God is love. He loves every single person he has made. He is neither vindictive nor cruel. The kindest, most loving thing he can do for people who don't want to live under the lordship of Jesus his Son is to bring their life to an end, and that is what he will do. But before doing that he will rectify every injustice that has not already been taken care of on earth. This will take the form of punishment in proportion to whatever evil has been committed. How long this will last is not stated, but it has to end before the creation of the new earth, when pain and death will be no more. (Revelation 21.1-4) Of one thing we can be sure: it will last no longer than necessary.

On the day of judgment the requirements of justice will be fully satisfied, just as they are on earth today whenever just rulers carry out their responsibilities properly.

Torment

Nevertheless, there are three passages in the New Testament which seem to say that the wicked, or at least some of them, will be everlastingly tormented, either after their first death or after the day of judgment.

(i) The rich man and Lazarus

In Luke chapter 16 Jesus told a story about an unnamed rich man and a very poor man named Lazarus who both died at about the same time. Here is part of the story:

> "The rich man also died and was buried; and in Hades, being in torment, he lifted up his eyes, and saw Abraham far off and Lazarus in his bosom. And he called out, 'Father Abraham, have mercy upon me, and send Lazarus to dip the end of his finger in water and cool my tongue; for I am in anguish in this flame. …send him to my father's house, for I have five brothers, so that he may warn them, lest they also come into this place of torment.' But Abraham said, 'They have Moses and the prophets; let them hear them.'" (Luke 16.22-29)

This story is rather strange:

- It is the only passage in the Bible that represents Hades or Sheol as a place of flames and torment. As we have seen,

Job wrote, "There the wicked cease from troubling, and there the weary are at rest. There the prisoners are at ease together" (Job 3.17,18). Other passages in the Old Testament tell us that there is no knowledge there, no remembrance of God or anything else, and no speaking (Ecclesiastes 9.10; Psalm 88.11,12). If Jesus meant this parable to be taken literally he would have been contradicting the word of God in the Old Testament. And nowhere else does Jesus himself describe Hades as a place of torment or even warn his hearers against ending up there.

- When Jesus told this parable everybody, rich and poor alike, went in spirit to Hades at their death, even the prophet Samuel (Job 3.19; 1 Samuel 28.3-19). So why did Lazarus go somewhere nicer?

- In the Bible the dead are always regarded as sleeping, i.e. unconscious, until they are resurrected on Resurrection Day or at the last judgment (Daniel 12.2; Matthew 9.24; 1 Corinthians 15.18; 1 Thessalonians 4.13-17). Yet as soon as the rich man died he and Abraham were conversing with each other.

- It suggests that Lazarus went to a place of blessing simply because he was poor.

- By describing the rich man as being in torment while his brothers are still alive, it suggests that judgment takes place the moment someone dies. However, the New Testament consistently says that the destiny of people who do not believe in Jesus won't be decided until the day of judgment.

- It suggests that disembodied souls have eyes, fingers and tongues!

The explanation is simply that it was a story Jesus made up, based on the beliefs of the Pharisees whom he was addressing. Almost every detail of this story can be found in Jewish writings in the Talmud and other literature current at the time. For example, in the Babylonian Talmud, Book II, folio 72, 'Kiddushin', it is said of a rabbi on the day of his death, "This day he sits in Abraham's bosom." Jesus told this story in terms that the Pharisees could accept in order to show them truths that they were not accepting.

The Sadducees once did exactly the same thing to Jesus. They didn't believe in any resurrection, but they told Jesus a fictional story about a woman who had seven husbands in turn, and then asked him whose wife she would be in 'the resurrection'. Just as they made up a story in terms of something they didn't personally believe, in order to get their point over to Jesus, so Jesus made up a story about the rich man and Lazarus in terms that he didn't believe, in order to get his point over to the Pharisees in terms that they could accept. Jesus told this story primarily to urge his audience to believe the teaching of Moses and the prophets, and to tell them that if they didn't do so then even when he rose from the dead they would not believe in him. He never intended it to be a factual account of what happens in the afterlife.

Sadly this parable has been influential in shaping an understanding of life immediately after death that is contrary to the Bible's teaching, including the false doctrine of purgatory.

(ii) Revelation 14.9-11

> If any one worships the beast and its image, and receives a mark on his forehead or on his hand, he also shall drink the wine of God's wrath, poured unmixed into the cup of his anger, and he shall be tormented with fire and sulphur in the presence of the holy angels and in the presence of the Lamb. And the smoke of their torment goes up for ever and ever; and they have no rest, day or night, these worshippers of the beast and its image, and whoever receives the mark of its name. (Revelation 14.9-11)

These verses describe the fate of people who surrender to the antichrist during the last three and a half years before Christ returns, not the fate of anyone who dies before then. We are told that those who worship the beast will be tormented with fire and sulphur by a wrathful God in the presence of Jesus and his angels; 'the smoke of their torment' will continue 'for ever and ever', and that they 'have no rest, day or night'. To understand all this we first have to understand how the various words and phrases are used elsewhere in the Bible:

- The Greek word *basanizō*, translated 'torment', normally means 'to vex with grievous pains of body or mind, to torment'. However in Revelation 18.9,10,15-17 John uses the same word 'torment' to refer to the destruction of Rome. (Revelation 17.1-12 makes it clear 'Babylon' is a pseudonym for the city of Rome. If John had openly encouraged people to accept the imminent destruction of Rome he could easily have been put to death as a traitor.) "And the kings of the earth … will weep and wail over her when they see the smoke of her burning; they will stand far off, in fear of her *torment_*... The merchants ... will stand far off, in fear of her *torment*, weeping and mourning aloud, 'Alas, alas, for the great city ... In one hour all this wealth has been laid waste.'" So in Revelation the word can refer to a relatively brief process of destruction.

• 'Fire and sulphur (brimstone)' is an expression used in the Bible for a principal means of destruction used by the Lord. "Then the Lord rained on Sodom and Gomorrah brimstone and fire from the Lord out of heaven; and he overthrew those cities, and all the valley, and all the inhabitants of the cities ..." (Genesis 19.24,25). "On the wicked [the Lord] will rain coals of fire and brimstone ..." (Psalm 11.6). "And the streams of Edom shall be turned into pitch, and her soil into brimstone; her land shall become burning pitch" (Isaiah 34.9). "... the heads of the horses were like lions' heads, and fire and smoke and sulphur issued from their mouths. By these three plagues a third of mankind was killed, by the fire and smoke and sulphur issuing from their mouths," (Revelation 9.17,18). The Lord sends fire and brimstone to produce destruction and death.

• The Greek word *orgē*, translated 'wrath', is used in the New Testament to mean 'God's anger at man's disobedience, obduracy (especially in resisting the gospel) and sin, which expresses itself in punishing the sinner'.[5]

---

[5] *A Greek-English lexicon of the New Testament.* Grimm's Wilke's Clavis Novi Testamenti, translated, revised and enlarged by Joseph H. Thayer, fourth edition, T & T Clark, Edinburgh, 1901.

An *earthly ruler acts on God's behalf in punishing wrongdoers: "... he does not bear the sword in vain; he is the servant of God to execute his wrath on the wrongdoer"* (Romans 13.4). In the Bible any ruler who did not punish the wicked would be regarded as a bad ruler who encouraged wrongdoing.

- 'The smoke of their torment will continue for ever' is a Biblical expression that means the associated destruction will be permanent. It may also contain the idea that the destruction will be permanently remembered. Prophesying the forthcoming destruction of the land of Edom, Isaiah wrote, "…its smoke shall go up for ever. From generation to generation it shall lie waste; none shall pass through it for ever and ever" (Isaiah 34.10,11). Clearly Edom did not burn for ever and the smoke of its burning did not go up for ever, but its destruction lasted for ever: it was a permanent destruction. In Revelation 19.3 a multitude in heaven celebrates the burning of Rome (see Revelation 18.8) with the words, "Hallelujah! The smoke from her goes up for ever and ever!" This did not literally mean that the smoke would rise for ever, for two chapters later John tells us that Rome and everything else in the present earth will pass away and God will make all things new (Revelation 21.1,5). The heavenly multitude probably meant that the destruction of Rome would never be forgotten.

- The Greek word *anapausin*, translated 'rest', means 'intermission', 'cessation', 'rest' or 'recreation'.

- 'Day *and* night' is a phrase used in the Bible to mean 'continuously'. "This book of the law shall not depart from your mouth, but you shall meditate on it day and night ..." (Joshua 1.8). "... his delight is in the law of the Lord, and on his law he meditates day and night" (Psalm 1.2). At the dedication of the temple Solomon prayed "... that thy eyes may be open day and night toward this house ..." (2 Chronicles 6.20). [6] 'Day and night' always means something that happens or is done continuously. (See also Psalms 32.4; 42.3; 55.10; 88.1.)

- 'Day *or* night' and 'day *nor* night' are phrases used in the Bible to refer to something that does not happen or is not done. "... neither day nor night one's eyes see sleep ..." (Ecclesiastes 8.16). "... neither eat nor drink for three days, night or day" (Esther 4.16). "It shall not be quenched night nor day ..." (Isaiah 34.10 KJV). 'Nor' is the correct translation of this verse in Isaiah, not 'and' as in the RSV.

These verses in Revelation 14.9-11 cannot mean that those who worship the beast will be tortured in flames for ever in the presence of the Lamb, for the Lamb is Jesus, and when Jesus comes to dwell on earth in the heavenly city, there will be no more crying nor pain in his presence (Revelation 21.4,22,23), and nothing and no one will be accursed any more (Revelation 22.3). Here are some further reasons.

---

[6] Revelation 20.10 says that the devil and his associates '*will be tormented day and night for ever and ever*'. In the coming ages there may not be days and nights as we know them, so in the book of Revelation at least the phrase 'day and night' doesn't necessarily mean two 12-hour units of time in this present age. It just means continuously.

- **Destruction**: As we have seen earlier, the fate of the damned is the permanent destruction of body and soul; it is not eternal life in any form. '*The wages of sin is death*' (Romans 6.23).

- **Everlasting joy:** To those whose names are written in the book of life God has promised to wipe every tear from their eyes, and that sorrow and sighing will be replaced by everlasting joy (Revelation 21.4; Isaiah 35.10). How could they be free from sorrow and sighing if they knew that unbelieving members of their families – perhaps even their own children – were everlastingly burning to death in flames of choking sulphur?

- **Vengeance:** God has said, "Vengeance is mine; I will repay," (Deuteronomy 32.35; Romans 12.19; Hebrews 10.30). God said this to stop people taking vengeance into their own hands, by promising that he would deal with wrongdoers himself. In 2 Thessalonians 1.5-9 Paul does indeed state that the Lord Jesus will inflict 'vengeance upon those who do not know God and upon those who do not obey the gospel of our Lord Jesus', but he immediately explains what form that vengeance will take: "They shall suffer the punishment of eternal destruction." The Greek words *olethron aiōnion* mean their permanent ruin, destruction or death. That is the principal vengeance that God will inflict on the disobedient, through his Son Jesus.

- **Justice:** "...all his ways are justice. ...just and right is he" (Deuteronomy 32.4). God himself laid down a rule that justice must be equitable: 'an eye for an eye and a tooth for a tooth'. (See Leviticus 24.17-20.) How then could he torment for ever someone who has been forced into worshipping an idol for no more than three and a half years in order to buy food for this children?

- **Ange**r: God's anger against sinners will not last for ever. "He will not always chide, nor will he keep his anger for ever" (Psalm 103.8,9).

- **Mercy:** God is merciful. "Be merciful, even as your Father is merciful" (Luke 6.36). Everlasting torture would by definition be unmerciful.

So what *do* these verses in Revelation 14:10-11 mean?

Using the explanations I have given above, the words …

> "he also shall drink the wine of God's wrath, poured unmixed into the cup of his anger, and he shall be tormented with fire and sulphur in the presence of the holy angels and in the presence of the Lamb. And the smoke of their torment goes up for ever and ever"

… mean that anyone who worships the beast will be justly and permanently destroyed by God in the presence of Jesus.
The second part,

> "and they have no rest, day or night, these worshippers of the beast and its image and whoever receives the mark of its name"

has to be correctly translated and punctuated in order to be understood. Although the RSV says 'day or night', the Greek says 'day *and* night'. As I've explained, 'day and night' always means something that happens or is done continuously, not something that doesn't happen, like not having any rest. Secondly, there was no punctuation in the original Greek text, so we have to decide from the context where one sentence ends and another begins. Although this second part begins with the word 'and', John begins at least half the sentences in this chapter with the word 'and', so it could easily be the start of another separate sentence. It would then literally be translated, '(And) they have no cessation day and night the ones worshipping the beast and its image and if anyone receives the mark of its name.' This new sentence is now a comment on the previous sentence. It explains that God's condemnation and sentence of death on these people is just because day and night without ceasing they worship the beast and its image. Their behaviour is the antithesis of the behaviour of the four living creatures around the throne of God in Revelation chapter 5. The four heavenly creatures never cease day or night to worship God!

> ... day and night they never cease to sing, "Holy, holy, holy, is the Lord God Almighty, who was and is and is to come!" (Revelation 4.8)[7]

So this second part of Revelation 14.9-11 is not about ceaseless torment, it is about the ceaseless worship of the beast worshippers, which justifies their death sentence.

---

[7] The Greek of Revelation 4.8 says, 'They do not have respite day and night they are saying holy, holy, holy' etc. The phrase 'day and night' describes what they *are* doing, not what they are *not* doing, just as it does in other Bible passages.

(iii) Revelation 20.9,10

The third passage in the New Testament about torment is in Revelation chapter 20. Two verses describe the fate of the human armies of the antichrist who will assemble to attack Jerusalem at the end of Christ's thousand-year reign, and the fate of the antichrist, the false prophet and the devil.

> And they marched up over the broad earth and surrounded the camp of the saints and the beloved city; but fire came down from heaven and consumed them, and the devil who had deceived them was thrown into the lake of fire and sulphur where the beast and the false prophet were, and they will be tormented day and night for ever and ever. (Revelation 20.9,10)

The most obvious meaning of these verses from the Revised Standard Version is that the human armies of the antichrist, together with the antichrist, the false prophet and the devil, will be tormented for ever in a lake of fire and sulphur. This presents two further problems.

Firstly, verse 9 says that the human armies will be consumed by fire. The Greek word translated 'consume', *katefagen*, means 'to consume by eating, to eat up, to devour; or to utterly consume or destroy by fire'. That can only mean the end of them. This contradicts verse 10, which seems to say they will then be tormented day and night for ever and ever. Happily there is a simple solution to this problem. As I said, the Greek text itself doesn't have any punctuation, and John often starts a sentence in Revelation with the word 'and'. So without changing any words, the two verses above should be punctuated as two separate sentences like this:

And they marched up over the broad earth and surrounded the camp of the saints and the beloved city; but fire came down from heaven and consumed them. And the devil who had deceived them was thrown into the lake of fire and sulphur where the beast and the false prophet were, and they (i.e. the devil and the beast and the false prophet) will be tormented day and night for ever and ever.

That is how these verses are punctuated in the Authorized Version, which in this case is correct. The devil, the beast and the false prophet will be perpetually tormented, but the human supporters of the antichrist will be destroyed.

However there is a second more serious problem in verse 10. If the devil, the beast and the false prophet are to be tormented continuously for ever that can only mean that they will exist for ever. Yet the letter to the Hebrews tells us that Jesus took on our human nature,

> ... that through death he might destroy him who has the power of death, that is, the devil. (Hebrews 2.14)

Similarly Paul wrote in 1 Corinthians 15.24 that when Jesus delivers the kingdom to God the Father at the end, it will be "... after destroying every rule and every authority and power", by which he meant the devil and all his angels. So whether Jesus is going to destroy the devil or destroy the devil and all his angels, the devil cannot continue to live for ever as Revelation 20.10 suggests. Moreover Paul said in 2 Thessalonians 2.8 that the beast will be destroyed too. *"... the Lord Jesus will slay him with the breath of his mouth and destroy him by his appearing and his coming"*, he wrote. The Lord will kill him and destroy every vestige of him. So how can Revelation 20.10 be true when it implies that the devil, the beast and the false prophet will live for ever?

Some people suggest that the Greek phrase *eis tous aiōnas tōn aiōnōn*, translated 'for ever and ever', could mean 'until the perfect age comes', when the torment of the devil and his collaborators would cease. The Greek word *eis* occurs hundreds of times in the New Testament but only in three verses[8] does it unambiguously mean 'until', and these are not in the phrase *eis tous aiōnas tōn aiōnōn*. The phrase *eis tous aiōnas tōn aiōnōn* occurs eleven times in the New Testament referring to God's eternity, where it can mean nothing other than 'for ever'. For example:

- ... our God and Father; to whom be the glory for ever and ever (Galatians 1.4,5);

- "... I died, and behold I am alive for evermore" (Revelation 1.18);
- ... to him who is seated on the throne, who lives for ever and ever (Revelation 4.9);
- ... God who lives for ever and ever (Revelation 15.7).

In such verses the phrase couldn't possibly mean merely 'until the perfect age comes'; it can only mean 'for ever'. That's how New Testament Greek says 'for ever'. So when we come to the only two other instances of the phrase in the Bible, one referring to smoke going up (Revelation 14.11) and the other referring to the torment of the devil, the beast and the false prophet (Revelation

---

[8] The three New Testament verses where *eis* means 'until' are Acts 25.21, 1 Thessalonians 4.15 and 2 Timothy 1.12.

20.10), it can only mean what it means everywhere else in the Bible: 'for ever and ever'.

As we saw earlier, the phrase 'the smoke of their torment goes up for ever and ever' is not intended in the Bible to be taken literally, except perhaps in the sense that the memory of it will endure for ever. So when Revelation 20.10 says that the devil, the beast and the false prophet will be tormented day and night for ever and ever, is that intended to be understood literally or not?

John Wesley adopted two principles in interpreting the Bible.

(i) "It is a stated rule in interpreting scripture never to depart from the plain, literal sense, unless it implies an absurdity", and

(ii) "The general rule of interpreting scripture is this: the literal sense of every text is to be taken, if it be not contrary to some other texts. But in that case, the obscure text is to be interpreted by those which speak more plainly."[9]

He mentioned both principles together in his sermon *A Call to Backsliders*:

It does not appear that we have any reason to depart from the literal meaning [of Hebrews 6.4] as it neither implies any absurdity, nor contradicts any other scriptures.[10]

If Revelation 20.10 were interpreted literally it would clearly contradict many other scriptures. So how else could it be

---

[9] From a letter written by Wesley to Samuel Furly.

[10] *A Call to Backsliders*. Sermon 86, I (4), 1778.

interpreted? Jesus's teaching gives us a clue. In order to highlight the importance of something that he was teaching, Jesus would sometimes express it in exaggerated terms. For example:

- "It is easier for a camel to go through the eye of a needle than for a rich man to enter the kingdom of God" (Mark 10.25). If he meant that literally then no rich man would be able to enter God's kingdom, and that would have excluded Abraham for a start.

- "If your right eye causes you to sin, pluck it out and throw it away … And if your right hand causes you to sin, cut it off and throw it away; it is better that you lose one of your members than that your whole body go into hell (Gehenna)" (Matthew 5.29,30). If Jesus meant that literally, then most of his disciples would have been physically disabled.[11]

- "… he who eats my flesh and drinks my blood has eternal life…" (John 6.54). He hardly intended that literally!

---

[11] I find it interesting that some Christians insist on taking literally the words about going to hell (actually the rubbish tip) but they never take literally the first part of the same sentence that says they should cut off their hand if it causes them to sin. It is intellectually dishonest to dismiss as figurative the words one doesn't want to believe and to insist on taking literally the words that for some reason one does want to believe. If Jesus meant the first part of the sentence figuratively is it so unreasonable to suggest that he meant the second part figuratively too?

- "But now … let him who has no sword sell his mantle and buy one" (Luke 22.36). On the way to his arrest Jesus warned his disciples of trouble ahead for them too. But when they replied that they did have two swords he immediately told them that two were quite sufficient: he hadn't literally meant them all to sell their precious coats and start killing people.

Paul could also exaggerate at times.

> … continue in the faith, stable and steadfast, not shifting from the hope of the gospel which you heard, which has been preached to every creature under heaven. (Colossians 1.23, literally 'which has been proclaimed in all creation under heaven'.)

When Paul wrote this around AD 61 he had not even reached Spain, and there is no evidence whatsoever that the gospel had been preached to every single inhabitant of Africa, Asia and America as well as to every animal, bird, fish and insect! I'm not going to suggest that the devil and his two collaborators will avoid torment altogether. If people who have engaged in genocide, torture and crimes against humanity will be punished in proportion to the suffering they have caused, then the antichrist and the false prophet will certainly be among them. And if wicked people will suffer, how much greater must be the torment that Satan and his demonic servants will have to suffer! That is why the demons asked Jesus, "Have you come here to torment us before the time?" (Matthew 8.29). But again, this period of divine retribution will not last for ever, for Jesus came to destroy the devil, and since the last enemy to be destroyed is death, once death has been thrown into the lake of fire only those whose names are written in the book of life will remain (Hebrews 2.14; 1 Corinthians 15.26; Revelation 20.14,15).

If the Lord Jesus and his apostle Paul could use exaggerated language, never intending it to be taken literally, why shouldn't John have done the same when he wrote that those three characters would be tormented for ever? John's passionate motivation in writing Revelation was to encourage believers in Christ to stand firm in their loyalty to Jesus even if it cost them their lives. It is likely that he wrote Revelation at a time when it was widely believed that Nero, the cruellest Roman emperor of all, was going to return from the dead and rule once again in the form of the antichrist.[12] John was desperately concerned that if those who had come to believe in Christ surrendered to the antichrist, they would lose their wonderful inheritance of eternal life in God's kingdom. He encouraged them to stand fast against the antichrist's demand for worship by reminding them in Revelation 14.9-11 of their fate if they gave in; and by assuring them in Revelation 20.10 that eventually the antichrist, the false prophet and even the devil would suffer the worst kind of fate possible. John wanted to provide them with a strong encouragement to stand firm in their newly found commitment to the true Christ. "Here is a call for the endurance of the saints, those who keep the commandments of God and the faith of Jesus", he wrote (Revelation 14.12). John deliberately used exaggerated language to emphasize the seriousness of his message, language that he did not seriously intend or expect anyone to take literally.

---

[12] *The Revelation of John, Volume 2*. W. Barclay, The Daily Study Bible, Revised Edition, The Saint Andrew Press, 1976. Commentary on Revelation chapter 13.

SUMMARY

SUMMARY

People who believe in Jesus, who put their trust in him as Saviour and live with him as their Lord, will not be among those present at the last judgment. They already have the promise of eternal life, and will be raised to everlasting life on the day of resurrection. Jesus said,

> "I am the resurrection and the life; he who believes in me, though he die, yet shall he live, and whoever lives and believes in me shall never die." (John 11.25,26)

Those who die not believing in Jesus as Saviour and Lord will be judged by their behaviour in the light of what they have known of God's will.

(i) **Death:** When they die their spirits enter Hades, the realm of the departed, in a state akin to sleep, to await the day of judgment.

(ii) **Judgment:** At the end of Christ's initial thousand-year reign over this present earth they will be resurrected, i.e. returned to a state of full consciousness in bodily form. In the presence of Jesus as judge they will then learn whether or not they are to be granted eternal life in God's kingdom.

(iii) **Salvation:** Those who have not knowingly rejected Jesus as Saviour, who have not lived manifestly wicked lives and died unrepentant, who have been kind to people in trouble, who have earnestly tried to live as good a life as best they know how, and who have been grateful to God for giving them life insofar as they have known him, will be granted eternal life in his kingdom.

(iv) **Damnation:** If they are not granted eternal life they will all experience extreme remorse. Some at least will then suffer some kind of painful retribution in proportion to whatever suffering they have caused on earth, for God is a God of justice, and he has promised to avenge wrong-doing, particularly the murder of his servants. (Romans 12.19; Deuteronomy 32.43; Revelation 19.2). Finally their life will be terminated for ever in what Revelation calls 'the second death', along with the devil and his angels.

The Bible does not teach that the destiny of the damned is to spend eternity being tormented in hell. Their destiny is annihilation. If the penalty of sin is to be everlasting torment then Jesus Christ did not suffer the penalty of sin in our place.

Most of us spend a lot of money insuring against events that will probably never happen. How much more sensible it is to insure against an event which most definitely will happen – the day of judgment. The one sure way to avoid standing before Jesus as judge on that day is to put your life now into his hands as Saviour.

"… he who hears my word and believes him who sent me,
has eternal life; he does not come into judgment,
but has passed from death to life."
(John 5.24)

"… therefore choose life, that you … may live!"
(Deuteronomy 30.19)

ALSO ON THIS SUBJECT

Hell and Judgment in the Book of Revelation

By Colin Sweet

There is a danger nowadays that Christians may either dismiss the reality of hell or, because of simply accepting traditional ideas on the matter, have a very limited and incorrect understanding of the subject.

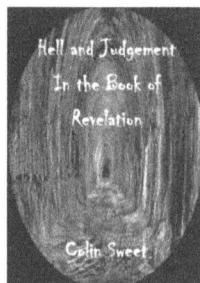

A full treatment would require a much lengthier exposition but the primary concern of this publication is the final destiny of unbelievers as it appears in the book of Revelation. Although he has limited his field of enquiry the author deals with many of the standard issues and in these pages all Christians will find much which stimulates.

Further details can be seen on **www.obt.org.uk**

Copies are available from that website and from

The Open Bible Trust,
Fordland Mount, Upper Basildon,
Reading, RG8 8LU, UK.

It is also avaialble as an eBook from Amazon and Apple and as a KDP paperback from Amazon.

Asleep in Christ

By Helaine Burch

In this book the author encourages the reader to seriously enquire into the nature of mankind and to consider their destiny after death.

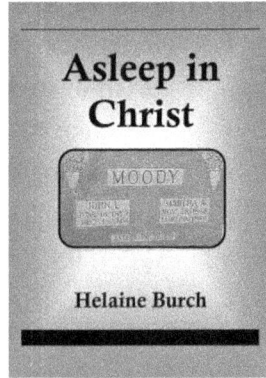

- Has man a soul, or is man a soul?
- What is 'soul'?
- What happens to the soul at death?
- What is the place of resurrection?

These basic questions, and many others, are discussed dispassionately using the Bible as the source for answers.

The Chapter headings are:

- What is death according to the Bible?
- Why does man die?
- The penalty of sin is death
- Jesus Christ, the solution to sin and death
- Faith is the key to eternal life
- Death is likened to sleep
- What is resurrection
- Resurrection will bring us into the presence of the Lord
- Now is Christ risen from the dead
- What is soul? (nephesh / psuche)
- What is spirit? (ruach / pneuma)
- What is hell? (sheol / hades)
- Hell and hell fire (Ge Hinnom / Gehenna)
- The fate of the unredeemed
- Hebrew words used to describe the penalty of sin –

perish/destroy/destruction
- Greek words used to describe the penalty of sin – perish/destroy/lose
- The Lake of fire and the second death
- Concluding comments
- Appendix 1 - The Rich man and Lazarus
- Appendix 2 - Problematic Scriptures
- Indexes

Further details can be seen on **www.obt.org.uk**

Copies are available from that website and from

The Open Bible Trust,
Fordland Mount, Upper Basildon,
Reading, RG8 8LU, UK.

It is also avaialble as an eBook from Amazon and Apple and as a KDP paperback from Amazon.

ABOUT THE
AUTHOR

Arnold Page is married to Ann and they have four children. He has been a Methodist minister, a researcher and lecturer in the field of timber engineering, and a published nutritionist. He founded the British charity 'Chile for Christ' following a period of missionary service in southern Chile.

ABOUT THIS BOOK

"How can a God of love deliberately torment unbelievers for ever in hell, especially if they have never heard of Jesus?"

That is a question many Christian writers fail to address. However, in this book Arnold Page faces it head on by showing, from the pages of Scripture, that God does not do such a thing, and that eternal torment is not the fate of unbelievers.

Indeed, some of them will have their names written in the Book of Life.

Contents include:

- The basis of judgment
- The fate of the unrighteous in the New Testament
- Death, destruction or perishing
- Gehenna, the Gehenna of fire, fire
- Weeping and gnashing of teeth
- Punishment
- Torment

Publications of The Open Bible Trust must be in accordance with its evangelical, fundamental and dispensational basis. However, beyond this minimum, writers are free to express whatever beliefs they may have as their own understanding, provided that the aim in so doing is to further the object of The Open Bible Trust. A copy of the doctrinal basis is available on **www.obt.org.uk** or from:

THE OPEN BIBLE TRUST
Fordland Mount, Upper Basildon,
Reading, RG8 8LU, UK

www.ingramcontent.com/pod-product-compliance
Lightning Source LLC
Chambersburg PA
CBHW060656030426
42337CB00017B/2639